A Book

Devotions to the Martyrs of England, Scotland and Wales

by Fr John S. Hogan

"We all have to experience many hardships before we enter the kingdom of God"

Acts 14:22

All booklets are published thanks to the generous support of the members of the Catholic Truth Society

CATHOLIC TRUTH SOCIETY

PUBLISHERS TO THE HOLY SEE

Image page 5: Stained glass in Our Lady and the English Martyrs Church, Cambridge *by Lawrence Lew OP (flickr).*

All rights reserved. First published 2017 by The Incorporated Catholic Truth Society, 40-46 Harleyford Road London SE11 5AY Tel: 020 7640 0042 Fax: 020 7640 0046. © 2017 The Incorporated Catholic Truth Society.

ISBN 978 1 78469 150 9

Contents

Introduction. 6

Prayer to Jesus, King of Martyrs 9

Prayer to Our Lady, Queen of Martyrs. 10

Prayer to St Andrew 11

Prayer to St George 12

The Pre-Reformation Martyrs. 13

St Alban, The Protomartyr. 13

Ss Julius and Aaron 15

St Oswald 17

St Winifred. 20

St Boniface 22

St Adrian of May 26

St Magnus of Orkney 27

St Thomas Becket 29

St William of Perth 33

The Reformation Martyrs 35

Prayers to the Martyrs of England and Wales 35

Blessed Margaret Pole. 38

St Philip Howard 40

St Anne Line. 41

St Edmund Campion 42

St Edmund Arrowsmith 44

4

St John Fisher.....................................46

St Thomas More....................................48

St Margaret Ward..................................51

Blessed John Roche................................53

St Margaret Clitherow.............................55

St John Kemble 56

Blessed Thomas Sherwood..........................57

Blessed George Douglas............................59

St John Ogilvie...................................60

The Martyrs of Wales **62**

Invocations to the Martyrs of Wales................73

Litany of the Welsh Martyrs.......................81

Novena of Humility to Blessed Humphrey Pritchard ..83

Prayer for the Young to Blessed Richard Flower......84

Stained glass in Our Lady and the English Martyrs Church, Cambridge.

INTRODUCTION

The slaying of the French priest, Fr Jacques Hamel in his church in the Rouen suburb of St-Étienne-du-Rouvray on the 26th July 2016 led to an outpouring of grief and a resurgence of emphasis on the nature of Christian martyrdom. Fr Jacques was the not first priest in recent times to be slain for his Catholic faith, indeed many hundreds have been martyred with thousands of the faithful; but his murder in a country of the industrialised, secularised West shocked many and led them to see his death not as an absurd or meaningless act, but one of supreme witness to Christ and the Gospel in the face of hatred and violence. In the midst of this re-evaluation of Christian witness unto death, spontaneous devotion sprung up leading to calls for Fr Jacques' canonisation. Time will tell if these calls are more than a momentary reaction, but the natural emergence of devotion is as ancient as the Church herself, as the faithful sense that a Christian who has been killed in *odium fidei* - in hatred of the faith, is worthy of veneration.

This veneration of martyrs is one of the earliest devotions in the Church. Following the various persecutions, Christians looked upon the martyrs as the great heroes of the faith, those who offered the supreme testimony to Christ and the Gospel by laying down their lives rather than renounce their Christian faith. Conscious that any of them could be asked to embrace a similar sacrifice, Christians fostered profound relationships with these Saints, commending to their intercession the trials and difficulties of life, and seeking strength to imitate these heroes should persecution break out upon them. Even if they were not called to renounce their lives through martyrdom, these devotees of the martyrs saw in the heroic deeds of their confreres lessons that could be translated into daily life: for their own humble witness to the Christian faith in the world and daily conversion to a life of virtue and holiness.

A new age of martyrs

Without doubt we ourselves now live in a new age of martyrs (as if martyrdom was ever absent from the Church), and so the lives and witness of the martyrs are as relevant now as in any other time. In such times, as Christ's disciples, we are called to bear the cross in a more radical way. In the midst of relentless attack and calumny, the example and intercession of the Church's martyr Saints and Blesseds provide comfort, companionship and encouragement. The Saints know us and love us; from heaven they look down on us and intercede for our needs. Whether we realise it or not they are involved in our lives, and most certainly so when we are suffering. In these times, as in the past, the Church urges us to look to these our brothers and sisters and, rather than lose heart, find strength and wisdom in their lives and friendship.

The holy martyrs offer us more than companionship. The blood of the martyrs does not seek vengeance for the acts that were committed against them. Rather it pleads with the God of mercy for the conversion of souls; for grace to be poured out upon the world because the blood of the martyrs is united to the Blood of Jesus Christ through which the world is redeemed. Their blood, then, has an extraordinary intercessory power and strength because of their sacrifice and their union with the Lord in his Passion. This is a spiritual strength we must harness in these difficult times.

Powerful intercessors

This little Book of Martyrs is intended to remind the faithful of some of these powerful intercessors from among those who lived and suffered on the island of Britain. Among the many Saints and Blesseds of England, Scotland and Wales are extraordinary figures who have a message for us today. They are as present to us now as they have been since the day they made the supreme sacrifice and took their place in the kingdom of heaven. Some are well known, others not so well known; but yet they all deserve to be acknowledged and venerated. They are already our intercessors and they accompany us on our earthly pilgrimage, praying for our needs.

At this time, a time when martyrdom could well be a reality for us, it is a worthwhile spiritual exercise to come to know these martyrs and foster a personal relationship with them. It is hoped that this little book will facilitate this and make known to the wider public these heroic men and women who faced the most awful of times with faith, hope and charity, trusting in the mercy of God and sustained by the vision Christ their Saviour laid before them and in union with him, offered themselves as a sacrifice for the salvation of the world.

Prayer to Jesus, King of Martyrs

My Lord and God, Lord Jesus Christ,
Merciful King, I worship and adore you,
for you took flesh
and offered yourself as an oblation
for the redemption of my soul.
Most sweet Martyr, Martyr of Martyrs,
Eternal Sacrifice of Grace,
accept this offering of my heart and soul,
which I dedicate to your service.
Receive me, O Lord, as an oblation,
offered in union with the blood of the martyrs;
accept, in reparation for my sins,
my sufferings, trials and difficulties.

O King of Martyrs, give me your grace,
transform me according to your will,
that I may be faithful and true;
that I may renounce myself,
take up my cross and joyfully follow you.
O Jesus, I trust in you.
Amen.

Prayer to Our Lady, Queen of Martyrs

O most holy Mother of God,
Queen, whose heart bears the wounds
of your martyrdom,
as foretold by holy Simeon;
intercede for your children
that in times of trial and difficulty,
they may always have the grace
and strength of your Son,
and with him triumph over all adversity.
Amen.

Prayer to St Andrew
The Holy Apostle and Patron of Scotland

O holy Apostle of the Lord, St Andrew,
the first to be numbered among those
who shared intimately in the life of Christ;
the first to bring to him those souls
in need of mercy and redemption,
offer me to the Lord
that he may grant me the graces I need
to embrace the Christian life in its fullness
and be for him a true witness
in the midst of the world.
By the holy cross on which you died
in imitation of our Lord and Saviour
teach me to make of my trials and sufferings
an oblation acceptable to him,
for his glory, for the salvation of my soul
and for the good of his holy Church.
Amen.

Prayer to St George
Martyr Patron of England

St George, blessed soldier of the Lord,
who, in imitation of our Saviour,
overcame the dragon
by offering your life in testimony
to the sufferings of Christ
and to his resurrection from the dead.
Hear us, great patron,
and protect those who turn to you.
May we be vested in holy charity,
confirmed in faith and hope
so true peace may reign in our hearts.
Obtain for us purity of mind and body,
so we may be made ready for the battles
that await us on our pilgrim way.
May Christ's victory shine forth in us
and his kingdom be made present
in our poor lives
and in the lives of all his faithful.
Amen.

THE PRE-REFORMATION MARTYRS

St Alban, The Protomartyr

According to numerous sources, St Alban is regarded as the first Briton to shed his blood for Christ, so he bears the title Protomartyr. Though little is known of his life, a number of sources relate the story of his martyrdom, notably St Bede the Venerable in his *History of the English Church and Peoples*.

Alban lived in Verulamium, what is now the southwest part of St Albans in Hertfordshire, during the Roman period, possibly around the turn of the third and fourth centuries. Alban was a pagan who gave shelter to a Christian priest, said to have been called Amphibalus, as he was fleeing persecution. Touched by the priest's vigil of prayer during the night, Alban experienced a conversion and in the following days the priest instructed him in the faith.

In the meantime the authorities had uncovered where the priest was hiding and soldiers were sent to Alban's home to capture him. When they arrived they found only Alban dressed in the priest's cloak and presuming him to be Amphibalus, arrested him and brought him before a judge who realised this man was not the priest. Furious with the impersonator, the judge told Alban that he would be condemned to receive the punishment the priest would have received, whereupon Alban confessed his Christian faith. Under interrogation when asked about his family, Alban replied, "If you wish to know the truth about my religion, know that I am a Christian, and carry out Christian rites". As the judge pressed him on his family and his name, Alban replied, "My parents named me Alban, and I worship and adore the living and true God, who created all things". The judge demanded that he offer incense to the Roman gods; when Alban refused he was flogged.

Steadfast under torture, he was beheaded on the banks of the local river. Before his death he converted his executioner and another had to be called to carry out the beheading. According to St Bede the martyrdom took place on the 22nd June, and though the year is disputed, some traditions date it around the year 287 while others place it within the Great Persecution of Diocletian, around the year 301. His feast is celebrated on the 20th June.

Prayer to the Protomartyr

Blessed Alban,
the first of the British
to shed your blood for Christ,
as you worshipped and adored
the true and living God
who created all things,
instil in my heart similar sentiments
of true devotion.

That my life may be offered each day
as an act of oblation to this Lord
who made me from earth
who redeemed me in his blood
who immersed me
in the waters of salvation.
Through your prayers
and blessed patronage
teach me how to serve him in this life
so I may glorify him forever in heaven.
Amen.

Ss Julius and Aaron

As with St Alban, one of our chief sources of information on the martyrdom of Ss Julius and Aaron is St Bede's *History*. Bede notes, at the end of his account of St Alban's martyrdom, "In the same persecution suffered Aaron and Julius, citizens of the City of Legions, and many others of both sexes throughout the land. After they endured many horrible physical tortures, death brought an end to the struggle, and their souls entered the joy of the heavenly City." The 'City of Legions' has traditionally being regarded as Caerleon-on-Usk in Wales, and while some scholars speculate it could be Chester or even York, the weight of evidence and tradition falls to Caerleon. Some legends maintain that they were Roman soldiers converted by the priest Amphibalus soon after he escaped Verulamium.

Some speculate that Aaron may have been a native Briton, and Julius, a Roman. Dying soon after Alban, they may have been victims of Diocletian's persecution. Nothing else is known about them. Their feast day is celebrated in Wales, with St Alban, on the 20th June.

Prayer to Ss Julius and Aaron

Your names shall live forever,
faithful disciples of Christ,
Ss Julius and Aaron,
teach us the way of hope,
that in the midst of the darkness
the light of faith, shining through us,
may console the people of our time.

Pray for us, O blesseds Julius and Aaron
That we may be made worthy of the promises of Christ

Let us pray

Almighty Father,
your martyrs, Ss Julius and Aaron,
touched by the life of the Gospel,
laid down their lives
in testament to your Beloved Son,
our Lord Jesus Christ.
Through their prayers,
immerse your people in your peace,
and fill their hearts with that hope

which consoled these blessed martyrs
in the midst of their sufferings.
We ask this through Christ our Lord.
Amen.

St Oswald

King Oswald of Northumbria, "a man beloved of God" according to St Bede, ranks among the great martyrs of England whose memory inspired an important cultus for many centuries. He was born around the year 604, the son of Æthelfrith, the ruler of Bernicia and Deria in Northumberland. When his father was killed in battle in 616 and an exiled member of the Derian royal family, his uncle, Edwin, succeeded him, Oswald and his family went into exile in Scotland. It was here that he came into contact with the monks of Iona and converted to Christianity.

In 633 King Edwin was defeated and killed in battle by Cadwallon ap Cadfan, the king of Gwynedd who, in an alliance with Penda of Merica, sought to take possession of the thrones of Bernicia and Deria. In the wake of Edwin's defeat, Oswald's brothers attempted to take back their kingdoms: Osric tried to establish himself in Deria, and Eanfrith took Bernicia. Cadwallon defeated both brothers and established his rule in the two kingdoms, first killing Osric, and then Eanfrith in 634 as he had attempted to negotiate peace with Cadwallon. Though Cadwallon was Christian, his rule was barbarous and for a year he governed his new kingdoms as a tyrant. To claim what he believed was his by right Oswald gathered a small army and confronted Cadwallon at Heavenfield. Before battle, he had a wooden cross set up facing over the battlefield and gathered his soldiers around it to pray for victory. Oswald and his little army prevailed and Cadwallon was killed.

Christian faith in the kingdom

Reuniting Northumbria, Oswald governed as king for eight years, becoming the Overlord for the other Saxon kings. One of his major concerns was the establishment of the Christian faith in his kingdom, inviting missionaries from Iona to preach the Gospel. Foremost among these was St Aidan with whom Oswald shared a close friendship, and to whom he gave the island of Lindisfarne in 635 to establish a new See. As at first Aidan spoke only Irish, Oswald acted as his interpreter when the bishop was preaching. He married Cyneburga, daughter of the king of Wessex. He had at least one son, Æthelwald, but it is uncertain as to whether he was the child of the marriage or from a previous relationship before Oswald's conversion. As king, St Bede notes, he was good, humble and generous. He had a great love for the poor, built several churches and gave land and endowments to establish monasteries.

Though Oswald had established peace, old enemies were not inclined to accept it, and King Penda of Mercia was as warlike as ever. At battle in Maserfield, on the 5th August

642 Oswald was killed. After the battle Penda, a pagan, wanted to offer the dead king's remains as a sacrifice to his god Woden, and so had the body dismembered. However most of the remains were not lost, and were gradually recovered and enshrined in various monastaries. Oswald's death was hailed as martyrdom and he was revered as a defender of the Christian faith. Miracles began to occur when he was invoked, and this led to his being declared a Saint. His feast day is the 5th August.

Novena of Courage
To St Oswald

Glorious St Oswald, defender of the faith,
we turn to you and ask that you intercede
with the true and living God,
that in his mercy, he may protect us
from the arrogant savagery of the enemy
and all his wiles and temptations.
Obtain for us from Christ our King
the grace of fortitude and holy fearlessness
so we may embrace our baptismal call
to heroism and holiness,
and fulfill our Lord's fervent desire
that we be pure salt, the light of the world,
warriors in the battle for the salvation of souls.
Amen.

St Winifred

Though she is not a martyr in real terms, St Winifred has enjoyed a widespread cultus down the centuries as a virgin and "honorary martyr" given her defence of her virginity. A niece of St Beuno, she was born in Tegeingl, Wales, in the early years of the seventh century, daughter of a chieftain, Tyfid ap Eiludd and his wife Wenlo. She was brought up Christian, and she was so devoted to her faith she decided to dedicate her life to God.

A suitor, Caradoc, the son of a neighbouring prince, was unconvinced by her plans and tried to persuade her to agree to marry him, but she refused. In a rage the young man attacked her. Legend maintains that he actually beheaded her, that she died *in defensum castitatis*, and as her head fell to the ground a well miraculously sprung up. Her uncle, St Beuno, in grief, prayed for her restoration and she was brought back to life. Following this miracle no one dared stand in the way of her plans, and so Winifred took the veil. Her suitor, Caradoc, according to legend, insolent and defiant, suddenly dropped dead and the ground opened up and swallowed him. However, other histories note that Winifred's brother Owain killed Caradoc in revenge for the attack on his sister.

Winifred entered a nunnery at Gwytherin, were she later became abbess and died with a reputation for sanctity. Her cult flourished and the site of her "martyrdom",

Holywell, became a place of pilgrimage. In 1138 her relics were translated to Shrewsbury. Accepting the legend and her "resurrection" many considered her an "honorary martyr". Though many doubt the veracity of the legend of her beheading, old accounts of her life make mention of a scar on the back of her neck, testifying to an attack of some sort. A comparable event occurred in the life of St Mariam Baouardy (1846-1878), the Palestinian Carmelite, who was almost beheaded in her youth as she defended her Christian faith and miraculously survived. It may be Winifred had a similar experience. St Winifred's feast is celebrated on the 3rd November.

Novena of Purity
Through the intercession of St Winifred

O gracious Lady, St Winifred,
who defended the chastity
you offered to the Lord
to the shedding of blood;
hear our prayer for your favour
and assist us in our struggle
to live lives of purity and virtue.
Help us overcome all temptations
so to remain pure of heart.
Salve our eyes with the vision of grace,
that they may resist impious curiosity.
Distract our minds

with memories of Christ's victory.
Turn our poor bodies to the strength
of the Most Holy Eucharist
where Christ our banquet burns away,
with gentle and ineffable love,
all sin and imperfection,
to immerse us in his consoling presence.
Help us, holy virgin of Christ,
to make of our lives and bodies
a living sacrifice for God.
O holy Winifred, sweet mother,
be our defender and aid.
Amen.

St Boniface

Among England's saints and martyrs is the Apostle of Germany, St Boniface, who crowned a long life of missionary service with martyrdom. Born in Crediton, Devon, around the year 675 and baptised Winfred, he was a member of a wealthy, influential and pious Christian family. From an early age Winfred wanted to spend his life in God's service, but his father opposed his entry into a monastery. Thanks to much prayer, the young man prevailed and he entered the monastery of Exeter. He was educated there and later at the Benedictine monastery of Nursling near Winchester. As a monk he became a teacher, and at the age of thirty he was ordained priest. He proved to be a successful teacher and preacher, and he was held in great esteem by important figures outside the monastery including the local king, Ina of Wessex.

In 716, when the Abbot died, he was nominated Abbot, but Winfred declined; he had his heart set on another ministry: missionary work. That same year he left for Frisia, now the northern Netherlands and north-eastern Germany, to preach the Gospel. Great difficulties and political problems made the missionary expedition incapable of carrying out the mission, so in 717 Winfred returned to Nursling where he was elected Abbot against his will. He declined the appointment and left the monastery for Rome in 718 to ask for a mandate to preach the Gospel as a missionary. Pope Gregory II granted the request, but for Hesse and Bavaria. The pope also gave him a new name: Boniface in honour of the martyr St Boniface of Tarsus. On his way to Germany, hearing conditions were now better in Frisia, and St Willibrord and his missionaries there were in need of help, Boniface made his way there and worked on the mission. In 722 he was called to Rome to be ordained bishop by the pope. Following his consecration he went to Germany to initiate what proved to be a very successful mission, converting countless souls.

Apostle of Germany

In 732 he was again called to Rome to receive the dignity of Archbishop of Germany and the pallium from the hand of

Pope Gregory III. When he returned to Germany his work bore tremendous fruit with the conversion of thousands. He founded numerous bishoprics and established the Church on a firm basis, thereby earning the title 'Apostle of Germany'. He was later made Papal Legate to Germany and as such called a major synod at which, among other things, he established a hierarchy in Bavaria. His responsibilities were increased when he was asked by Rome to conduct a reform of the Church in France which was in serious decline. Presiding over reforming councils from 742 to 747, and filling vacant dioceses and encouraging a renewal in faith, he brought the Church in France back to life. For all his efforts, which were monumental and helped shaped Western Europe, Boniface endured many difficulties both in Germany and France where he discovered his greatest enemies were not pagans, but lapsed Christians who were resentful of his reforms and success.

Boniface's arduous work continued unabated until he reached the age of eighty when he resigned his responsibilities in Germany and France, ensuring his offices were given to trustworthy and evangelical pastors. Now free, rather than live a life of retirement, he set himself to take up his original missionary work in Frisia. When he arrived back he discovered that he had to reclaim some areas he had evangelised many years before, which he did successfully, and then began missionary work in areas not yet touched by Christianity. It was while he preparing for a confirmation ceremony on the banks of the river Borne, near Dokkum, on the 5th June 754, he was set upon by pagans who killed him and his companions. His body was taken to Fulda and enshrined there. His feast is celebrated on the 5th June.

Prayer for Zeal
Through the intercession of St Boniface

O Boniface,
disciple and apostle of the Gospel,
instil in our hearts that zeal
which led you to win souls for Christ
and sustained you
as you shed your blood for love of him.
Gentle pastor,
may we be set aflame
with evangelical fire,
that we may become the Gospel in flesh
and touch the hearts of all men and women
to draw them to Christ.
Amen.

Let us pray

Heavenly Father, through the intercession
of your fervent disciple, St Boniface,
who spent himself in the service of the Gospel
and shed his blood for its proclamation,
plant in our hearts the seed of zeal,

and with your grace, nurture it so it may grow
and become a great tree to shelter us in holiness
and make us fit to serve, with utter selflessness,
the cause of your kingdom.
Through Christ our Lord.
Amen.

St Adrian of May

St Adrian, also called Ethernan, was a monk of the monastery on the island of May, off the coast of Scotland. Little is known of his origins, though some accounts claim he was Irish. According to some traditions he was Bishop of St Andrews, who after founding a number of monasteries, fleeing the raids of the Danes and drawn to the contemplative life himself, he settled on May. In 875 he and the community were martyred at the hands of the Danes who ransacked the monastery. Adrian and the community were buried in a common grave. The island later became a centre for pilgrimage with a shrine dedicated to him. His feast is celebrated on the 4th March.

Prayer to St Adrian
For the conversion of souls

O Blessed Adrian, faithful soul,
who fell beneath the blows
of those who knew neither Christ
nor the salvation he offers,
intercede that our hearts

may turn to our Lord and Saviour
in daily conversion.
Filled with the grace of his Spirit
pray that our lives may testify
to his presence in the world
and his saving work for all.

O loving Christ, may your desire
that all men and women be saved
be fulfilled.

Lord Jesus, save souls.

St Magnus of Orkney

St Magnus was born on Orkney in 1080, the son of Erlend Thorfinnsson, a Norse earl and co-ruler of Orkney with his brother Paul. When the island was invaded by the King of Norway who made his illegitimate son Sigurd earl, Magnus and his cousin Haakon, Paul's son, were taken into the service of the king. Converted to Christianity, he refused to take part in Viking raids on Anglesey, remaining on ship praying the psalms, earning a reputation for gentleness and piety. Escaping to the court of the King of Scotland, Magnus lived a penitential life, eventually returning to Orkney to share governance with his cousin Haakon in 1105 as earls. By 1114 tensions which had arisen exploded among followers of the earls. War was avoided by an agreement to negotiate on the island of Egilsay at

Easter 1116. However Haakon arrived with vastly superior troops intent on murdering Magnus. The saintly earl took refuge in a church, but was captured and killed with an axe blow to the head. He died offering his life as a sacrifice and praying for his killers. He was buried at the spot where he died. Though his death was most likely a political killing, he was acclaimed a martyr and miracles occurred at his grave. His feast is celebrated on the 16th April.

Prayer in the midst of suffering
Through the intercession of St Magnus of Orkney

Receive, most Blessed Father,
these my pains and sufferings,
which I offer with all my heart,
united to the Passion and death
of your beloved Son,
Jesus Christ our Lord.
Through the intercession
of your martyr St Magnus,
who in selfless love offered up his death,
grant me the graces of endurance,
peace of mind and generosity of heart.
May what I bear be of service to you
and your holy Church.
Amen.

St Magnus, be my companion in my trials,
my advocate in my distress.

St Thomas Becket

One of the most venerated martyrs in the medieval Church, St Thomas Becket was born in Cheapside in London on the 21st December 1118. He was educated first at home and then from the age of ten at the Augustinian Priory at Merton. In his free time he mingled with his father's wealthy friends, often spending time at the country estate of Richer de L'Aigle where he was introduced to hunting and hawking. At the age of twenty he spent a year in Paris continuing his education. Due to his father's financial problems, Thomas's schooling ended and he found work as a clerk first under a businessman and later in the household of Theobald of Bec, the Archbishop of Canterbury.

The Archbishop recognised the young man's abilities and sent him to Bologna and Auxerre to study canon law. When he returned, Theobald entrusted him with various missions which Thomas successfully completed. Ordaining him deacon, Theobald appointed him Archdeacon of Canterbury. In this position Thomas came into King Henry II's circle and revealing his various talents and abilities, he became a favourite of the king. In 1155 Henry appointed Thomas as Chancellor of England, and so began his immersion in the affairs of state and his deep friendship with the king. Thomas embraced a more worldly life, was known for his lavish entertainment, his sporting prowess but also his efficiency and capabilities. Though no saint at this time, he was pious and chaste, and did not neglect the simple spiritual formation his mother taught him.

The defence of the Church

In 1162, following the death of Theobald of Bec, Thomas was elected Archbishop of Canterbury. Since he was a deacon he had to be ordained priest before his episcopal consecration. This and his new office seemed to have affected a change in him. He adopted a more personally austere way of life, wearing a hairshirt under his clothes, taking the discipline, spending more time in prayer and offering vigils at night. Though he was still a magnificent entertainer and as determined as ever, this change in his personal life was noted by Henry who had hoped their relationship would continue as before. Henry had engineered Thomas's election so he could have greater control of the Church. Thomas, however, was determined to carry out the duties of his state and this included the defence of the Church from state interference. He resigned the Chancellorship of England, and he worked to recover the rights and freedom the Church had lost to the state. This brought him into direct conflict with Henry and as the next few years passed their relationship soured. While Henry maintained he was merely seeking his rights as established under his father's reign, Thomas rejected this and a bitter struggle ensued. Thomas's followers were persecuted and he was eventually driven into exile in France.

He spent six years in exile in France, living in various monasteries and participating in the life of the monks. Spiritually this time was of great benefit to him. While he and the king engaged in a war, both men appealed to Pope Alexander III to intervene. The pope was cautious in the extreme, and while he knew that, for all his faults and impetuousness in dealing with Henry, Thomas was correct, he tried to find a compromise. Henry was vindictive and sought Thomas's ruin while Thomas imposed censures on the king's episcopal supporters. Neither was prepared to give way, but after six years Henry agreed to a compromise and an uneasy reconciliation was brokered in 1170 allowing Thomas to return to Canterbury.

However, an issue regarding the coronation of young Prince Henry, the heir to the throne, emerged. By right, only the Archbishop of Canterbury conducted coronations, but King Henry had chosen another bishop, an ally, to crown Prince Henry. In response Thomas excommunicated the bishop. Enraged the king uttered rash words, "Who will rid me of this turbulent priest?" Four knights of the court took the king at his word and left for Canterbury. Arriving on the 29th December 1170, after an altercation with the Archbishop, they killed him in the cathedral as he was making way to the choir for Vespers. Immediately after his death miracles began to occur at his tomb, and he was canonised in 1173. His feast day is the 29th December.

Prayer for the Church
Through the intercession of St Thomas Becket

Holy martyr of God, St Thomas Becket,
as your blood washed the cathedral of Canterbury,
so now offer your prayers for the Church
that the Eternal Father may bless her and renew her,
and wash her children clean in the Blood of Christ.
Pray that her bishops and priests may be true shepherds,
consecrated in the truth and immersed in charity,
proclaiming the Word of God with pure zeal
and seeking the salvation of souls.

Intercede, O blessed Thomas,
that she may be purified and strengthened
to shine as a beacon in the darkness,
so, as Mother to orphans, enflamed by the Spirit,
she may lead all men and women to the heart of Christ
and to the embrace of our Heavenly Father.
In the midst of sufferings, console her;
in the midst of temptations, pray for her;
in the midst of sinfulness, shake her;
in the midst of confusion, guide her.
Assist her, sweet shepherd of Christ,
with your fervent intercession.
Amen.

St William of Perth
(St William of Rochester)

St William was born in Perth and was a fisherman by trade (though some accounts claim he was a baker). Following a conversion experience in his youth, he became a devout man attending Mass daily and assisting local orphans and the poor. One day he found an abandoned baby boy at the church door; he adopted the boy, called him David and raised him. Having made a vow to make the pilgrimage to Jerusalem he set out around the year 1201 with David as his companion. As they were passing through Rochester, for some reason David turned on William, cut his throat and robbed him. His body was found by a woman suffering mental illness and following her miraculous healing the local monks buried William in the cathedral where other miracles occurred. In 1256 the Bishop of Rochester recognised him as a martyr since he had been killed as he was on pilgrimage and successfully petitioned Rome for his canonisation. A great shrine emerged, second only to Canterbury in medieval England. He is the patron saint of adopted children. His feast day is the 23rd May.

A Parent's Novena to St William of Perth
For children

Receive these little ones, O blessed William,
and watch over them by night and by day.
Lead them to Christ, so they may find in him
a true friend, a worthy confidant, a wise teacher.
Guide my heart, my mind and my will,
my every deed, my work and my rest,
so open to the promptings of the Holy Spirit,
I may raise these children entrusted to me
with a Christian soul and a loving heart.
Pray that I may be attentive to the weakest,
and never losing faith,
face the challenges which lie ahead
with quiet confidence in God
and the maternal intercession of our Mother Mary.

O St William, sweet martyr,
I commend to your care these, my children,
so they too may know the measure of love.
Amen.

THE REFORMATION MARTYRS

Prayers to the Martyrs of England and Wales

Novena Prayer to the Martyrs of England and Wales

To you, Holy Martyrs of England and Wales, we commend our prayers and our needs in these difficult times.

As you laid down your lives for Christ and His Church, we ask that we may emulate your sacrifice in our daily lives, living as true and humble disciples of Christ.

May His Gospel so penetrate our minds and hearts that we may become what He urges us to be: salt of the earth and light of the world, making Him present through holy lives to the men and women of our time.

Sustain us with your loving presence, be our companions on our earthly journey.

Defend us in moments of trial, console us in sorrows and remind us of that joy which Christ implants into the souls of His devoted servants.

Intercede that we may truly be servants of mercy and reconciliation.

Watch over us and guide us in our Christian lives so one day we may merit to be with you in the Kingdom of our Heavenly Father.

Amen.

All you Holy Martyrs of England and Wales, pray for us.
That we may be made worthy of the promises of Christ.

Let us pray

Almighty God, who in our country raised up martyrs from every walk of life to vindicate the authority of your Church in teaching and worship, grant through their intercession, we pray, that all our people may be gathered once again to celebrate the same sacraments under the one Shepherd, Jesus Christ your Son. Who lives and reigns with you in the unity of the Holy Spirit, one God forever and ever. Amen

Memorare
To the English and Welsh Martyrs

Remember, O most faithful servants of God,
you holy martyrs of England and Wales,
that in your trials and persecution
the Lord listened to your pleas
and came to assist you in your needs.
I now turn to you and urgently recommend
myself to you. Do not refuse to listen to
my prayer, O blessed patrons of my cause,
but in your loving kindness
grant me your protection and help.

Novena of Forgiveness
Through the intercession of the English and Welsh Martyrs

Lord Jesus, you have told us to forgive those who have offended us seventy times seven. In your mercy, through the intercession of the holy martyrs of England and Wales, grant us the grace to forgive and not to count the cost, for we ourselves have received abundantly from the treasures of your mercy.

> Our Father. Hail Mary. Glory be.
> Lord Jesus, have mercy upon us.

Lord Jesus, from the cross you prayed "Father, forgive them, they know not what they do". In your mercy, through the intercession of your holy martyrs, grant us the grace to respond in charity to those who have offended us, remembering that we ourselves have received from the fountain of your gracious kindness.

> Our Father. Hail Mary. Glory be.
> Lord Jesus, have mercy upon us.

Lord Jesus, you have said that we must forgive those who have offended us from our hearts. In your goodness, through the intercession of the holy martyrs, grant us the grace of renouncing anger for those who offend us, but seek reconciliation and peace with all our hearts, for we ourselves have been restored through the shedding of our Blood.

> Our Father. Hail Mary. Glory be.
> Lord Jesus, have mercy upon us.

Prayer of Resolution

Most Holy Trinity, Father, Son and Holy Spirit, before you, and the entire court of heaven, relying on your grace and the prayers of the Most Blessed Virgin Mary, my Mother, and all your Saints, most particularly the Holy Martyrs of England and Wales who forgave their persecutors from their hearts, I now resolve to forgive all those who have offended me, in particular N. I desire to forgive, and now I am resolved to live according to that desire, seeking reconciliation and peace. For you, O God, in your gracious mercy, have forgiven me my many transgressions and restored me to your friendship. May grace and mercy abound. Amen.

Blessed Margaret Pole

Blessed Margaret was born on the 14th August 1473, the daughter of George, Duke of Clarence and his wife Isabel Neville, she was one of the last members of the Royal House of Plantagenet. In 1487 she was married to Sir Richard Pole, cousin of King Henry VII, and they had five children, one of whom became Cardinal Reginald Pole. Widowed in 1509 and out of royal favour, she struggled to provide for her children in straitened circumstances, eventually turning to the charity of the Bridgettine nuns of Syon Abbey. In the midst of her trials she maintained a deep and trusting faith. When Henry VIII succeeded his father he restored Margaret to favour and appointed her governess to Princess Mary; he also permitted her to inherit her late brother's title. As Countess of Salisbury she was peeress in her own right, rare at that time, and an independently wealthy woman. A keen supporter of Queen Katherine of Aragon, Margaret opposed Henry's divorce and religious revolution, for which she was arrested in 1538. Condemned for her adherence to Roman Catholicism, she was imprisoned for two years in the Tower of London and finally executed on Tower Green on the 27th May 1541. Sentenced to be beheaded, due to the incompetence of the executioner and her own refusal to co-operate, she was butchered before her head was taken off.

Prayer in Need to Blessed Margaret Pole

O Blessed Margaret hear my prayer.
In your life you suffered poverty and deprivation,
loss of friends and loneliness,
yet in the midst of these trials
you placed your in trust in God.
In the midst of revolution and fear
you remained true to the Faith,
bearing neglect, hunger and illness
with great resolve and serenity,
finally shedding your blood
for the sake of Jesus Christ and his Church.
Pray for me, dear Margaret,
that I may not lose hope,

but in my sufferings, trials and darkness
that I too may turn to the Lord
and find my refuge in him.
Intercede that my faith may be strengthened,
my love deepened, my hope rekindled.
O holy Margaret, remember me,
be my friend and advocate
before the throne of God.
Assist me with your wise counsel,
And as I now place my cause in your hands,
Show me the way of wisdom, peace
and holiness. Amen

St Philip Howard

Born in London on the 28th June 1557, St Philip Howard was the son of Thomas Howard, 4th Duke of Norfolk and Lady Mary FitzAlan. Baptised Catholic, he was raised a Protestant, and from a young age became a favourite of Elizabeth I. With his father's fall from grace for supporting Mary, Queen of Scots, and his execution, the Howard family lost their titles, but Philip inherited his mother's father's title of Earl of Arundel. Married to Anne Dacre when he was fourteen he saw little of her, preferring a dissolute life at court. After hearing of St Edmund Campion and his fate, a change took place and he returned to his Catholic faith and his wife. In an effort to flee England in 1585 to live his faith, he was captured at sea and confined to the Tower of London. Condemned to death in 1589, he remained languishing in the Tower, expecting to be executed every day. He died of his sufferings and deprivation on the 19th October 1595.

Novena of Patience
Through the intercession of St Philip Howard

Grant us, Blessed Philip, your intercession, that we may, like you, endure all things for love of Christ. That in our hearts we may joyfully pray that the more affliction we endure for Christ in this world, the more glory we shall obtain with him in the next. Pray that our lives in this world may abound to his glory, and that we may serenely embrace his holy will. Obtain from him, for us, the gift of holy patience and constancy, the virtue of prudence and the strength of determination, so that in all things we may be sustained in faithful discipleship. Amen.

St Anne Line

St Anne was born Alice Higham around 1563 to a Puritan family in Essex. In the 1580s she and her brother William converted to Catholicism, and not long after she married Roger Line, also a Catholic; from the time of her marriage she was known as Anne. The three moved to London to live their Catholic faith more intensely and to assist the suffering Church there. In 1585 while assisting at Mass Roger and William were arrested; Roger was sent into exile and died abroad in 1594. Anne sought work as a maid, but renounced it to work in houses of refuge for priests, eventually running there such houses. Well known for her recusancy, her home was raided at Candlemas 1601 while Mass was being celebrated. Ensuring the priest escaped, Anne was arrested and committed for trial. Condemned to death at the Old Bailey for her activities, she was hanged at Tyburn on the 27th February 1601.

Novena of Charity
Through the intercession of St Anne Line

True servant of charity, St Anne,
pray for us that we, like you,
may the greet the stranger as Christ;
feed the poor, as Christ;
clothe the naked, as Christ;
tend the sick, as Christ;
visit those in prison, as Christ;
love our neighbour, as Christ;
pray for our enemies, as Christ;
lay down our lives, as you did,
in the service of holy charity.
Amen.

St Edmund Campion

Born in London on the 25th January 1540, Edmund Campion was considered a star in the various positions he embraced in his lifetime. He attended Oxford

University where he impressed Queen Elizabeth I with his oratory during her visit there and quickly became a favourite. Ordained a minister in the Church of England, he first sought promotion but his ambitions waned as he reflected on Catholicism. After helping found Trinity College in Dublin, he converted to Catholicism, eventually fled England and enrolled in the English College at Douai. In 1573 he was admitted to the Jesuits; he was ordained in 1578. He returned to England in 1580 to carry out an extraordinary ministry which led to his eventual capture on the 17th July 1581. Tried at Westminster Hall and found guilty of treason, he was hanged, drawn and quartered at Tyburn on the 1st December 1581.

Prayer for Evangelisation
Through the intercession of St Edmund Campion

Pray, O blessed Edmund, glory of England,
that the Holy Gospel of Jesus Christ,
so rooted in our ancient land,
may once again renew our people.
Pray, O holy martyr and evangelist,
that the holiness of our Saints
and the prayers of our ancestors
may inspire the servants of Christ here,
that He may reclaim this country as dowry
for the Queen of heaven.
Amen.

St Edmund Arrowsmith

St Edmund was born in Haydock, Lancashire, in June 1585 to a devoted Catholic couple. After a difficult childhood in which he tasted persecution, he left for Douai where he studied for the priesthood. Ordained priest in 1612, he returned to his native Lancashire to serve persecuted Catholics where he was zealous in his work and renowned for his forthright teaching. In 1623 he was arrested, but later released in an unofficial amnesty. In 1624 he entered the Society of Jesus. Betrayed by members of his own flock in the summer of 1628, he was brought to trial on the 26th August. After a travesty of a trial he was condemned to death and suffered martyrdom in Lancaster on the 28th August, being hanged, drawn and quartered. Since his martyrdom he has become renowned for his intercessory power.

Novena to St Edmund Arrowsmith

Faithful disciple of Christ, Holy St Edmund,
as with zeal you endured great suffering
and with true charity forgave your oppressors,
in your gracious kindness hear my prayers
and assist me in my needs.
The Lord has worked marvels through your prayers,
now with confidence in your powerful intercession
I commend my supplications to you…………
Through your example, dear St Edmund,
inspire me with a love for the Gospel

and the desire to live a holy life,
so like you I may be faithful and true.
Watch over me, sweet martyr of Christ,
and take me to your heart. Amen.

Thaumaturgus Prayer
to St Edmund Arrowsmith

Stretch out your holy hand to us,
blessed martyr of Christ,
St Edmund, faithful and true,
and intercede for us poor sinners
who are in need of God's holy grace,
that He may work miracles in our sight.

Prayer of Offering
(For the dying)
(Adapted from the Prayer of Offering of St Edmund Arrowsmith)

O Jesus, my life and my glory,
I cheerfully restore the life I have received from you,
and, was it not your gift,
would not be mine to return.
I have ever desired, O God of my soul,
to resign my life to you and for you.
My sins, O Lord were the cause of your death.
In my death I only desire you, who are true life.
Permit not, most merciful Jesus,
that I escape torments to live without you.
Life can be no advantage without you.

Give me, good Jesus, constancy to the last moment,
let me not live one moment without you,
for since you are true life, I cannot live
unless you live in me.
When I reflect that I have offended you
I am seized with greater grief than can be caused
   by the loss of my life.
O life of my whole life, have mercy on me.

I wholly devote myself to you,
and with all my heart I forgive those
who have offended me.
Have mercy on me, O Good Jesus.
I resign my life into your sacred hands.
God's holy will be done.

St John Fisher

St John Fisher was born in Beverly, Yorkshire, on the 19th October 1469. A brilliant young man, he was sent to Cambridge where he achieved a Master of Arts while studying for the priesthood. After ordination he carried out pastoral work and taught at Cambridge. He was later appointed chaplain to Margaret Beauford, Countess of Richmond and Derby, the mother of King Henry VII. Awarded a doctorate, he was appointed Vice-Chancellor of Cambridge University in 1501, and later Chancellor. Austere and a little stern at times, he was admired for his holiness, learning and goodness. As Henry VIII sought a divorce from his wife, St John was a defender and counsellor of

Queen Katherine of Aragon. When he refused to concede to Henry's religious revolution, he was condemned to death. For his heroic witness Pope Paul III created him a cardinal in May 1535. On the 22nd June of that year he was beheaded on Tower Hill. Originally sentenced to hanging, drawing and quartering at Tyburn, Henry revised the sentence fearing a riot following public outcry at St John's condemnation.

Prayer to St John Fisher

Beloved Shepherd, St John Fisher,
you are one of those of whom the Lord said
"You are the men who have stood by me
faithfully in my trials"
and now he has conferred a kingdom on you.
In your kindness remember us disciples
who still walk this pilgrim path.
Be our companion on the way of the Gospel,
intercede that we will be found trustworthy
and true to the Lord's commands.
Guide us to that wisdom that will transform us
and make us holy.
As you defended the innocent
and proclaimed the truth,
stand by us in all our trials and difficulties.
Pray for our needs, as we now commend them
to your intercession ....
O blessed John, martyr of the Lord,
be our constant patron and friend. Amen.

Prayer for the Shepherds
Through the intercession of St John Fisher

We commend to your watchful care,
O Holy St John, our dear shepherds.
Keep them true to Christ
so they may preach the Gospel in its fullness,
and be true fathers to their people
leading them on the way of authentic discipleship.
Obtain from the Lord the courage they need
to fulfil the duties of their office.
Pray that they may be tender and loving pastors.
When they fall through human weakness,
intercede that they may rise again
renewed in the Blood of Christ
and the grace of their ordination.
Be their constant companion, blessed John,
and lead them to win souls for Christ,
so they and all the faithful
may come to share in eternal glory. Amen.

St Thomas More

St Thomas was born in London on the 7th February 1478, the son of a lawyer, a profession he himself embraced, though he had considered a vocation to the London Charterhouse. Married twice, he was a loving father who educated all of his children equally and set them an example of pious Christian living. Famous for his sound scholarship, he was a leading voice in the Humanist movement. Holding a number of important offices, he succeeded Cardinal Wolsey as Lord Chancellor of England in October 1529, though he found the exercise of his office difficult at a time when Henry was breaking from Rome. Refusing to co-operate with the king's reformation, he resigned the office in May 1532 and retired to his home in Chelsea. Though he kept silence, his refusal to publicly support King Henry led to his arrest and his condemnation. Following a travesty of a trial, on the 1st July 1535, he was beheaded on Tower Hill on the 6th July.

Prayer to St Thomas More

Gracious St Thomas, joyful servant of Christ,
keep us in your heart,
and pray for us poor children of God
that we may embrace virtue and piety
and make his kingdom present on earth.
O blessed martyr of the Lord,
be our intercessor in this life,
help us through our difficulties,
to endure all things for love of Christ,
so that one day we may all merrily meet
to rejoice in the house of our Eternal Father
forever and ever. Amen.

Conscience Prayer
Through the intercession of St Thomas More

O blessed prophet, St Thomas More,
pray that we may stand secure
in the way of right conscience,
faithful to the Commandments
as revealed by God,
and the teachings of Jesus Christ
as preserved in the holy Catholic Church.
May we resist all efforts for us
to renounce our faith
and conform our consciences
to the whims and passing fashions
of the world.
Help us, most holy martyr Thomas,
that with true humility and faith,
we may seek the wisdom
which guides us on the way of truth.
Amen.

Prayer for Married Couples and the Family
Through the intercession of Ss John Fisher and Thomas More

From the beginning, Eternal Father,
you blessed the union of man and woman
in the bond of holy matrimony,
rooting it in the sacrificial love of Christ
and immersing it in sacramental grace.

Hear now, most gracious Lord,
the prayers of your martyrs,
Ss John Fisher and Thomas More,
as we commend to their intercession
the cause of marriage and family life.
They shed their blood in defence of marriage
and in witness to the truths taught by your Church;
now, we pray you, by the merits of their sacrifice,
united to that of your Beloved Son,
pour out your blessings on married couples
and upon their children.
Sustain those who, like these blessed martyrs,
proclaim your truth in these difficult times,
and help them bear their sufferings,
so, by means of their faithful witness,
they may touch the hearts of their persecutors
and draw all men and women
to the beauty of the truth.
We ask this through Christ our Lord.
Amen.

St Margaret Ward

Humble and good, innovative and pure, St Margaret was born in Congleton, Cheshire, though little else is known of her life. She came to London to seek work and was taken into service by a wealthy Catholic lady. Devoted to priests, St Margaret began to visit Fr William Watson who had been imprisoned in the Bridewell for his faith. As she gained the trust of the guards, she hatched a plan to help the priest escape. When she discerned the time was right she smuggled a rope into the priest and told him to climb out in the middle hours of the next morning. At about 2am, an Irish servant, Blessed John Roche awaited the priest in a boat. As the rope was not long enough the priest crashed down onto a shed, alerting the prison guards. Blessed John managed to get the priest and spirit him away to safety. When the rope was discovered, suspicion fell on St Margaret. She was arrested, tried, found guilty and hanged at Tyburn on the 30th August 1588. Blessed John Roche was later discovered and condemned to hang with her and other Catholics who had been found guilty of helping priests, the young Welsh martyr Blessed Richard Flower among them. They all died singing hymns.

Prayer to St Margaret Ward

You chose the better part, St Margaret,
pray that I too may choose this path:
that forgetful of self, I may devote my life
to the joyful service of my Lord and neighbour.
With you may I proclaim the Holy Name of Jesus,
be his humble and faithful witness in the world,
and offer myself as an oblation to his glory.
Amen.

Blessed John Roche

Blessed John Roche was born in Ireland and at some point in his youth came to London to find employment. He found work as a waterman and a servant. Raised a devout Catholic, he continued to practise his faith and was involved in the relief of priests with St Margaret Ward. He is known to have operated under the alias John Neale. In 1588, with St Margaret, he helped a priest escape from the Bridewell prison. He was later arrested and condemned to death for his faith. Offered a full pardon if he would ask the queen's forgiveness and attend a Protestant service, he refused. He was hanged with St Margaret and other Catholics at Tyburn on the 30th August 1588. As he is counted among the English Martyrs, he is also venerated among the Irish. In England and Wales his feast day is the 4th May; in Ireland his feast is celebrated on the 20th June.

Prayer for the Dispossessed
To Blessed John Roche

O Blessed John, take into your gentle heart
all those who are deprived;
those who have been dispossessed
of their homes and family,
the means to live or their dignity;
those who suffer under the yoke of oppression,
and those who have lost hope.
Intercede before God
that what has been taken from them

may be restored;
that they may put their trust in him.
Be their champion and their help,
and inspire us, disciples of the Lord Jesus,
to be Christ to them.
Amen.

Prayer for Immigrants
To Blessed John Roche

Holy John, faithful servant of the Lord,
in your life you had to leave family and native land
to seek work in another country,
enduring the hardships and discomforts of emigrants.
Remember now all those
who must endure the same trials and difficulties.
Accompany them on their journey
and bring them to a safe haven and place of refuge.
Guide them on their way,
help them in their troubles,
comfort them in their sadness and trials,
and pray that hearts may be opened to receive them.
For in receiving them, Christ is received;
in feeding them, Christ is fed;
in housing them, Christ finds a home;
in loving them, Christ is loved.
Blessed John, lead them to true apostles of charity
who will embrace them as Christ seeks to be embraced.
Amen.

St Margaret Clitherow

St Margaret was born in York in 1556, the daughter of a chandler. In 1571 she married John Clitherow, a butcher who lived in the Shambles. She was a loving wife, a devoted mother of five children and a conscientious neighbour. Though brought up Anglican, she converted to Catholicism in 1574 and thereafter offered her home and resources to assist the persecuted Catholics of York, with the blessing of her husband. Among her most daring works was her protection of priests, and she gained a reputation as the foremost activist in the North. When her son Henry left England to study for the priesthood, the family fell under greater suspicion than usual, and she was denounced for hiding fugitives. Brought to trial in 1586 she refused to plead to protect her husband and children, and so was condemned to '*peine forte et dure*', to be crushed until she confessed, or die in the process. Although found to be pregnant with her fourth child, St Margaret was pressed to death on Good Friday, the 25th March 1586.

Prayer of Supplication to St Margaret Clitherow

O Pearl of York, bright jewel of Christian England,
beloved wife and mother, refuge of the persecuted,
I commend myself to your prayers.

O blessed Margaret, true daughter of the Church,
pray that my heart is ever open to Christ

so I may find true sustenance in the Gospel,
comfort in his holy mysteries,
and authentic joy in the sacraments.
Be my companion on the way of discipleship
and instruct me on the life of virtue and self-denial.

Intercede for my needs, and pray before the Lord
for the request I now place in your hands.............
By your prayers, St Margaret,
help me be a true witness to Christ in the world.
May he triumph in me, so I may rejoice in him.
Amen.

St John Kemble

St John Kemble was born in Herefordshire in 1599 into
a prominent Catholic family. Leaving England in his
youth, he travelled to the English College at Douai where,
after studies, he was ordained priest on the 23rd February
1625. Returning to his native Herefordshire he took up
pastoral ministry there and in Monmouthshire. While
little is known of his fifty-three years faithful service,
he had many admirers and friends, both Catholic and
non-Catholic. In 1678 he was arrested and charged with
complicity in the Popish Plot, a fiction invented by Titus
Oates. Taken to London for interrogation, he was cleared.
However, being known to be a priest, he was charged
and tried. Found guilty, he was condemned to death. It
was decided that the sentence should be carried out in

Herefordshire, so he was returned to his native county. On the morning of the 22nd August 1679 he was informed he was to die; in response he asked for time to say his prayers, after which he took a drink and a final smoke of his pipe. Due to the incompetence of the executioner he was hanging for half an hour before he died; his body was then drawn and quartered.

Prayer for Serenity
Through the intercession of St John Kemble

St John, beloved priest of Christ,
intercede that in the midst of distress and trial,
the Lord may protect us from all anxiety and fear.
May that same serenity that filled your heart
throughout your life and bitter sufferings,
conquer us and lead us to a greater trust
in Christ our Saviour.
Amen.

Blessed Thomas Sherwood

Blessed Thomas was born in London in 1552, a member of a faithful Catholic family. When still young he took up a position of woollen draper, but in his heart discerned a vocation to the priesthood. After making arrangements to leave England, he travelled to Douai in 1576 where he was admitted to the English College. His financial situation insecure, he returned to London in 1579 to settle some affairs and obtain money to complete his seminary training. During his time at home he attended Mass at the home of a recusant lady, but he was later recognised by her Protestant son and denounced. Arrested and brought before a judge to answer charges, he refused to support the queen's supremacy and was taken to be tortured. Though every effort was made to make him reveal information about London's Catholics, Thomas remained silent. After a quick trial, he was condemned to death. For his stubbornness and refusal to co-operate with the authorities rather than being hanged, he was sentenced to be hanged, drawn and quartered. He died at Tyburn on the 7th February 1579 at the age of twenty-seven.

Prayer for Vocations
Through the intercession of Blessed Thomas Sherwood

Blessed Thomas,
pray that the Lord may raise up
men and women to offer their lives
in the service of the Gospel
and the mission of the Church.
Remember those who have been called,
that they may respond with generosity
and courage,
to joyfully embrace the path
the Lord has laid out for them.
Teach them how to surrender

to the will of God,
as you, in humble obedience and love,
laid down your life for Christ.
In your prayer, dear martyr,
pray that the Lord may sustain them,
and pour his graces upon them.
Amen.

Blessed George Douglas

Born in Edinburgh, little is known of Blessed George's early life. He came to England where he worked as a schoolmaster in Rutland. Over his years of teaching he discerned a vocation to the priesthood and eventually travelled to Paris where he entered a seminary. He was ordained priest in Notre Dame Cathedral. He was ministering in the north of England when he was arrested and arraigned for his priesthood. He was hanged, drawn and quartered at York on the 9th September 1587.

Novena for Wisdom
To Blessed George Douglas

Hear my prayer, O Blessed George.
In the moment of examination
you found the wisdom to proclaim Christ
even before your accusers,
so now intercede for me,
that the Spirit of wisdom

may dwell in my heart and guide me,
most especially in this concern

_____ .

Holy teacher, faithful priest, heroic witness,
be my advocate and friend. Amen.

St John Oglivie

St John was born in Banffshire, Scotland in 1579, and brought up a Calvinist. When he was sent to study at the University of Louvain he encountered Catholicism and converted in 1596. In 1600 he entered the Society of Jesus in Brno and was ordained priest in Paris in 1610. He ministered first in Austria and Rouen in France, but sought permission to return to Scotland which was granted in 1613. He was intent on making his way to Glasgow, arriving into England disguised as a horse trader, calling himself John Watson. He ministered for a year in Glasgow and Edinburgh, making numerous converts and earning a reputation among the authorities for his forthright preaching. Betrayed by man feigning conversion, John was arrested in October 1614. Tortured for months, he refused to renounce his faith and was condemned to death. He was hanged, drawn and quartered at Glasgow on the 10th March 1615. As he was pushed from the ladder to hang, he threw his rosary into the gathered crowd. It was caught by one of his enemies who, it was said, subsequently converted to Catholicism.

Novena of Hope to St John Ogilvie

In the midst of darkness, O dear St John,
pray that the light of Christ's hope
may enlighten our lives
and guide us on the way of truth
with confidence and peace.

O blessed martyr, St John Ogilvie,
apostle of holy hope, pray for us.

Rosary Prayer to St John Ogilvie

O blessed martyr, St John Ogilvie,
commend us to the heart of Mary,
Queen of the Holy Rosary,
that through her wise counsel
she may draw us more deeply
into the holy mysteries of Christ.

The Martyrs of Wales

Blessed Edward Powell

Born in Wales around the year 1478, Blessed Edward studied at Oxford University, gaining an MA and a doctorate in Divinity. Ordained a priest, he served in a number of appointments. A preacher to the royal court, he was held in great esteem by King Henry VIII who asked him to write a reply to Martin Luther's theology which he did in 1523. For this work he was praised by Oxford University and dubbed "the glory of the university". When the matter of the validity of Henry's marriage to Katherine of Aragon was being debated, Blessed Edward defended the bond and was a councillor to the queen. When he was accused by Hugh Latimer of insulting him, Blessed Edward was denounced to Thomas Cromwell, falling into royal disfavour. His fate was sealed when he refused to accept the legitimacy of Henry's union with Anne Boleyn. Attained for high treason he refused to take the Oath of Supremacy and was condemned by a Bill of Attainder. He was hanged, drawn and quartered at Smithfield on the 30th July 1540.

St Richard Gywn

St Richard was born in Llanidloes, Montgomeryshire in Wales around 1537. As a young man he went to Oxford to study, but later changed to St John's College, Cambridge. Following the accession of Elizabeth I in 1558, and the downfall of the College Master, his mentor, who was Catholic, Richard had to leave without obtaining his degree. He made his way to Douai to complete his studies. Returning to Wales, he devoted his life to teaching, first in Wrexham and then Overton. He married another Catholic, Catherine, and the couple had six children. At first he was a church-papist, a Catholic at heart, but attending Protestant services to cover himself. However, his Catholic sympathies became known to the local Anglican bishop who tried to make Richard and his family conform; this resulted in a campaign of harassment against the Gywns, forcing them to move house a number of times. The incident, however, led Richard to repent of church-papism. In 1579 he was arrested by the Anglican vicar of Wrexham who tried to force him to conform. Richard managed to escape and was on the run for the next year and a half. Recaptured in 1581, the authorities tried to force him to attend Protestant services, but he disrupted them and was fined for his refusal to attend and for brawling. In 1583 he was indicted on charges of treason and brought to trial. He was sentenced to death by hanging, drawing and quartering and was executed in Wrexham on 15th October 1584.

Blessed William Gunter

Little is known of Blessed William's life and ministry. Born in Raglan, Monmouth, he went to Reims and was ordained priest in 1587. Returning to England he carried out his ministry for just a year before being arrested in London in 1588 and imprisoned in Newgate. He was brought to trial for his priesthood with a number of others in the aftermath of the defeat of the Spanish Armada. The authorities were seeking retribution, and Blessed William and his companions were the fodder. Condemned to death, on the 26th August 1588 he was brought to Shoreditch where a new gallows had been erected outside a theatre. He was not permitted to speak, but immediately hanged, drawn and quartered. Among those who witnessed his martyrdom was St Robert Southwell.

Blessed Richard Flower

Blessed Richard was born in Anglesey in Wales in 1566. Though little is known of his life, this young man made his way to London and seems to have been living and working there. His older brother, Owen, was a priest, having been ordained in Cambrai in 1578 and was working on the English mission. Richard was a devoted Catholic himself and he was involved in serving and hiding priests. He was described by his accusers as "the chieftest reliever of priests" which testifies to his zeal. He is known to have used a number of aliases - among them 'Richard Lloyd', and also the surnames Fludd and Graye. In 1588 he was charged, with others, of assisting a priest, Fr William Horner - he had been hiding the priest in St Dunstan's in London. Found guilty, he was hanged at Tyburn with St Margaret Ward and other Catholic men found guilty of the similar crimes, on the 30th August 1588; he was twenty-one years old. As he and the others went to their death, they did so with great joy and serenity, singing hymns.

Blessed Humphrey Pritchard

Like Blessed Richard, little is known of Blessed Humphrey's life. He was born in Wales and worked in Oxford in an inn owned by a Catholic widow, the Catherine Wheel Inn on St Giles's, as a server. He may have been converted to the faith by this lady, but he proved to be a strong and zealous, assisting her in protecting and caring for priests. One day in 1589, priest hunters raided the inn as Mass was being celebrated; two priests were present. All were arrested and brought to trial. Blessed Humphrey was condemned to death for assisting priests in contravention of the law. On the 5th July 1589 he and his companions were led to the gallows on what is now Broad Street, Oxford. When his turn to be hanged came, he spoke to the crowd, "I call all people here present to bear witness, in this world and on the Day of Judgement, that I die because I am a Catholic, a faithful Christian of Holy Church". Some in the crowd mocked him for his ignorance and lack of education, to which Humphrey replied, "What I cannot explain by mouth, I am ready and prepared to explain and testify to you at the cost of my blood".

Blessed Edward Jones

Born in Lyndon, Blessed Edward was brought up Protestant, but converted to Catholicism. He travelled to Reims where he studied for the priesthood and was ordained in 1588. Returning to England he quickly gained a reputation as a holy man and an eloquent and powerful preacher among the faithful. For two years he evaded capture, his youth allowing him to pass for a student. With Blessed Anthony Middleton, he was hunted down by priest hunters, arrested and brought to the Tower of London where he was tortured. At his trail he defended himself brilliantly, but it was not enough to save him. While he was condemned to death, the court complimented him on his courage and eloquence. He was hanged, drawn and quartered in Fleet Street, London on the 6th May 1590.

Blessed William Davies

Born possibly in 1555 at Croes-yn-Eirias in Denbighshire in North Wales, his father is believed to have conformed to the Anglican faith, but William and other members of the family remained Catholic. He studied at Douai and Reims and was ordained priest in 1585. Returning to Wales he was arrested as he stepped ashore, but was freed soon after. He worked as a missionary for seven years, caring for recusant Catholics and teaching the faith. He secretly set up a printing press to produce Catholic books in Welsh, the first being his *Y Drych Christianogawl* (The Christian Mirror). In 1592, as he was escorting four young men making their way to seminary via Ireland, he was arrested at Holyhead. Initially separated from them, he managed to persuade his jailer to allow him visit them each day to offer Mass for them and continue their formation. Renowned as a holy and wise man, Catholics visited him in prison to seek his counsel and prayers. For the last six months of his life he was incarcerated with the seminarians and they lived a common life of prayer and study. He was hanged, drawn and quartered at Beaumaris, Anglesey on the 27th July 1593. The four seminarians were eventually released and made their way to the continent where they were ordained.

St John Jones

Born in Clynnog Fawr in Gwynedd, Wales, St John was brought up Catholic. He discerned a vocation to the religious life and entered the Franciscan Order in Greenwich and engaged in his formation until the community's dissolution in 1559. Leaving England he made his way to a house of the Order in Pontoise, France, and there he took the vows and was ordained priest. A number of years later he went to Rome and joined the Roman province of the *Reformati*, a strict branch of the Franciscans. In 1591 he asked his superiors to send him to England, but fearful of the dangers they hesitated until the following year when they relented. St John arrived in England in either late 1592 or early 1593, settling in London, but travelling to other parts of the country to carry out his work. During this time he was elected Minister Provincial by the English Franciscans. In 1596 he was captured and tortured. For two years he was imprisoned; during this time he met St John Rigby and converted him. On the 3rd July 1598 he was charged with going over the seas to be ordained, a crime in the Elizabethan statutes. Found guilty he was hanged, drawn and quartered on the 12th July 1598 at Southwark.

St John Roberts

St John was born in Trawsfynydd, Snowdonia, North Wales in 1577, into a Protestant farming family. Initially studying with a former local monk, he went to St John's College, Oxford in 1595, and from there to study law in London. Taking time to travel in Europe he became better acquainted with Catholicism and was received into the Church in Notre Dame Cathedral in Paris in 1598. Moving to Spain, he entered the Benedictine Order in Valladolid, making his profession in 1601. Ordained priest the following year in Salamanca, he was sent on the English mission on the 26th December 1602 and arrived in England in April 1603. Appointed vicar of the English monks of the Spanish congregation, he carried out pastoral work until he was arrested in July 1604 and banished. Exiled for fourteen months, which he spent founding a Benedictine monastery in Douai, he returned to England in October 1607 and continued his work. Arrested again the following December, he escaped and hid in London for about a year. Caught again in May 1609, he was incarcerated in Newgate prison and tipped for execution. Thanks to the intercession of the French ambassador, the death sentence was commuted to banishment. Visiting Spain and Douai, he made plans to return to England, and did so less than a year later. On the 2nd December 1610 he was arrested again just as he was finishing Mass in a safe house. On the 5th December he was tried and condemned to death, and on the 10th December he was hanged, drawn and quartered at Tyburn.

Blessed Philip Powel

Blessed Philip was born on the 2nd February 1594 in Trallong, Brecknockshire, Wales into a Catholic family. He was educated at Abergavenny Grammar School from where he went to study law at the Inns of Court in London. After a few years practising law, he left England for Douai where he entered the Benedictine Order in 1614. In 1618 he was ordained priest. In 1622 he returned to England to work on the mission in the West Country, serving as a priest for Catholics in general and then later as chaplain for a Catholic family. With the outbreak of the English Civil War, he became a chaplain to Catholic soldiers in General Goring's army in Cornwall. When the army disbanded he took a ship for Wales, but it was captured on the 22nd February 1646 and falling under suspicion, he was arrested. Brought to trial on the 9th June of that year, he was found guilty of being a priest and condemned to death. When he heard the sentence he exclaimed, "Oh what am I that God thus honours me and will have me to die for his sake?" and asked for a glass of sherry. He was hanged, drawn and quartered at Tyburn on the 3rd August 1646.

St Philip Evans

St Philip was born in Monmouthshire in 1645 into a Catholic family. He left Wales for St-Omer before going to Watten in Northern France where he entered the Society of Jesus on the 7th September 1665. He was ordained priest in Liège in 1675 and sent to back to Wales. Basing himself in the south, he carried out an intense ministry for four years. When the persecution resulting from the fictional Titus Oates Plot increased the risks, despite the faithful's pleas, St Philip remained and continued his work. On the 4th December 1678 he was captured at Sker, Glamorganshire and presented with the Oath of Alligance; refusing to take it, he was brought to Cardiff Castle and imprisoned. He was consigned to solitary confinement until another priest was incarcerated in the same cell, St John Lloyd. The two priests were brought to trial on the 5th May 1679 and found guilty. Condemned to death, both priests were executed by being hanged, drawn and quartered at Cardiff on the 22nd July 1679.

St John Lloyd

St John was born in Brecon in 1630, also the son of a Catholic family. He went to Ghent in Belgium to study humanities, but went to Valladolid to study for the priesthood. He was ordained on the 7th June 1653, and returned to Wales the following year. For the next twenty-four years he ministered to the Catholics of the country before being captured on the 20th November 1678. He was committed to Cardiff Castle, sharing a cell with St Philip Evans and becoming his companion at trial and in martyrdom. He was the second to die on the 22nd July 1679 having absolved and consoled his brother priest.

St David Lewis

St David was born in Abergavenny, Monmouthshire, in 1616, the youngest son of a Protestant minister. Though his mother was Catholic and had brought her other children in the faith, David was brought up a Protestant and was devoted to that faith. When he was sixteen he visited Paris as a law student, and it was there that he converted to Catholicism. Following the death of his parents, he left Wales for the English College in Rome for studies. He was ordained priest on the 20th July 1642. On 16th April 1644 he entered the Society of Jesus, and was appointed Spiritual Director to the English College in Rome. In 1648 he was sent to South Wales where he worked on the mission for thirty-one years. His ministry was marked by a deep love for the sick and poor, so much so that he became known as "the father of the poor". On the 17th November 1678 he was arrested as he was preparing to celebrate Mass. Condemned at the Assizes in Monmouth, he was condemned to death, and then sent to London for interrogation. Returned to Monmouth, he was hanged, drawn and quartered at Usk on the 27th August 1679.

Invocations to the Martyrs of Wales

Antiphon: O blessed sons of David, you who, by the Blood of Christ in which your blood was mingled, overcame the fire of the dragon. Rejoice now in your victory, and lead all souls on the way of truth.

Invocation I To Blessed Edward Powell

"But he who does what is true comes to the light, that it may be clearly seen that his deeds have been wrought in God". (*Jn* 3:21)

We invoke you, Blessed Edward, tender and learned pastor, defender of the faith, witness to the truth of Christ's teaching. O servant of the truth, pray that we may generously embrace and live the truth of Christ.

Hear us, O Father, blessed and faithful. In your mercy, through the intercession of your priest, Blessed Edward Powell, form the hearts of your children in fidelity to the Gospel.

Invocation II To St Richard Gywn

"Set me as a seal upon your heart, as a seal upon your arm; for love is strong as death, jealousy is cruel as the grave". (*Sg* 8:6)

We invoke you, St Richard, good husband, loving father, dutiful teacher, in the midst of tribulation you remained faithful. O model of conjugal life, pray that all husbands and wives may rejoice in their blessed union.

Hear us, O Father, loving and wise. In your mercy, through the intercession of your faithful son, St Richard Gwyn, confirm in your grace those children of yours united in the Sacrament of Marriage.

Invocation III To Blessed William Gunter

"For the oppressed let the Lord be a stronghold, a stronghold in times of distress." (*Ps* 9A:10)

We invoke you, Blessed William, servant of Christ the priest, who like him was offered on the cross of ungodly rage. O faithful servant of the sacraments, in the face of injustice, may we disciples of Christ be filled with charity.

Hear us O Father, just and true. In your mercy, through the intercession of your martyr-son, Blessed William Gunter, protect the innocent from the wrath and sinfulness of their oppressors.

Invocation IV To Blessed Richard Flower

"How wise you became in your youth! You overflowed like a river with understanding. Your soul covered the earth." (*Si* 47:14-15a)

We invoke you, Blessed Richard, flower of youth, ardent in charity, "chiefest reliever of priests". O patron of the young, pray that our hearts may be filled with an evangelical fire.

Hear us, O Father, tender and kind. In your mercy, through the intercession of your youthful martyr, Blessed Richard Flower, fill our young people with the fragrance of your love.

Invocation V To Blessed Humphrey Pritchard

"He guides the humble in the right path, He teaches his way to the poor." (*Ps* 24:9)

We invoke you, Blessed Humphrey, honest servant, generous disciple, most just man. What you could not say in words, you sealed with your blood. O humble son of the Most High God, pray that we may generously offer the work of our lives for the glory of our loving Lord.

Hear us, O Father, our Creator and sustainer. In your mercy, through the intercession of your humble son, Blessed Humphrey Pritchard, fill the hearts of your children with a spirit of generosity and kindness.

Invocation VI To Blessed Edward Jones

"Your word is a lamp for my steps, and a light for my path". (*Ps* 118: 105)

We invoke you, Blessed Edward, eloquent preacher of the Word of God, devout soul, teacher of the faithful in the way of holiness. O courageous martyr for the Gospel, pray that we may become true witnesses to Christ by our living his Word.

Hear us, O Father, teacher and master. In your mercy, through the intercession of your ardent preacher, Blessed Edward, grant us the grace to open our hearts to the fullness of your revelation, so we may transformed by your living Word.

Invocation VII To Blessed William Davies

"Whoever receives one such child in my name receives me; and whoever receives me, receives not me, but the one who sent me." (*Mk* 9:37)

We invoke you, Blessed William, fatherly defender of the young, zealous pastor, wise counsellor. Not even the chains of imprisonment could silence your ministry. O tender priest of Christ, keep in your heart those called by God to serve and obtain for them courage and determination.

Hear us, O Father, our helper and our strength. In your mercy, through the intercession of your zealous priest,

Blessed William Davies, grant courage and clarity to those children you are calling to serve in your Holy Church.

Invocation VIII To St John Jones

"My vows to the Lord I will fulfil before all his people. O precious in the eyes of the Lord is the death of his faithful." (*Ps* 115:14, 15)

We invoke you, St John, dear son of St Francis, consoler of the persecuted, soul serene and pure. With great patience you endured your torments and offered them as an oblation to Christ our Saviour. O soul consecrated to God, pray that we may live to the full the life we received at Holy Baptism.

Hear us, O Father, almighty and steadfast. In your mercy, through the intercession of your consecrated son, St John, renew in the hearts of your Religious the joy of their consecration.

Invocation IX To St John Roberts

"Into your hands commend my spirit. It is you who will redeem me, Lord." (*Ps* 30:6)

We invoke you, St John, son of Benedict, servant of the sick, comfort of the dying. You counsel us to remember our end for we shall all stand before the judgement seat of God. Grant us your blessing, O holy monk, and pray that our lives may be fruitful in faith and good works.

Hear us, O Father, our Judge and our defender. In your mercy, through the intercession of your joyful servant, St John Roberts, strengthen in faith and hope your children who are preparing to leave this life.

Invocation X To Blessed Philip Powel

"All these things my hand has made, and so all these things are mine," declares the Lord. "But this is the man to whom I will look, he that is humble and contrite in spirit, and trembles at my word." (*Is* 66:2)

We invoke you, Blessed Philip, fervent missionary, exemplary religious, awe-filled servant of the Light. You were filled with joy and gratitude when you were granted the honour to die as our Saviour died. O holy guardian of souls, pray that we may be filled with thanksgiving and praise of God

Hear us, O Father, our King and our God. In your mercy, through the intercession of your gracious priest, Blessed Philip Powel, guide in your truth those committed to serving your people in public life, that they be selfless in their service and dedicated to what is right and good.

Invocation XI To St Philip Evans and St John Lloyd

"How good and how pleasant it is, brothers dwelling in unity" (*Ps* 132:1)

We invoke you, blessed brothers in the holy priesthood, Ss Philip and John, devoted shepherds, companions in death, heirs to eternal life! The fragrance of your ministries rises to God and obtains every blessing for Wales. O holy pastors, pray that we disciples of Christ may grow in fraternal love for each other.

Hear us, O Father, gracious and forgiving. In your mercy, through the intercession of your priests, St Philip Evans and St John Lloyd, unite all your children in the bond of charity.

Invocation XII To St David Lewis

"Let your priests be clothed with holiness: your faithful shall ring out their joy" (*Ps* 131: 9)

We invoke you, St David, father of the poor, dedicated minister to those who suffer, strong and brave. You urge us to live holy Christian lives so one day we may share in the vision of God. O Servant of love, faithful pastor, pray that Sweet Jesus may receive our souls and form us according to his will.

Hear us, O Father, holy and gentle. In your mercy, through the intercession of your tender priest, St David, bless and sustain in their holy vocation our brothers who serve in the sacred priesthood.

Antiphon: O blessed sons of David, you who, by the Blood of Christ in which your blood was mingled, overcame the fire of the dragon. Rejoice now in your victory, and lead all souls on the way of truth.

Pray for us, you Holy Martyrs of Wales
That we may be made worthy of the promises of Christ.

Let us pray

Almighty Lord and Father you raise up your devoted sons, the Martyrs of Wales, for their constancy in faith, generosity in love and dedication to your Holy Church. Grant through their intercession that we your people may grow in holiness and joy, imitating their example and seeking the reconciliation of all your children. We ask this through Christ our Lord. Amen.

Litany of the Martyrs of Wales

Lord have mercy
Christ has mercy
Lord have mercy

Christ hear us
Christ graciously hear us

God the Father of heaven, *have mercy on us*
God the Son, Redeemer of the world, *have mercy on us*
God the Holy Spirit, *have mercy on us*
Holy Trinity, One God, *have mercy on us*

Holy Mary, *pray for us*
Holy Mother of God, *pray for us*
Our Lady of the Taper, *pray for us*
Queen adorned with the Light of Christ, *pray for us*

St Richard Gwyn, Faithful husband and father,
Teacher in the way of virtue, *pray for us*

St John Jones, Humble son of St Francis,
Teacher in the way of consecration, *pray for us*

St John Roberts, Devoted father to the sick and dying,
Teacher in the way of charity, *pray for us*

St Philip Evans, Defender of the flock of Christ,
Teacher in the way of constancy, *pray for us*

St John Lloyd, Faithful steward of the mysteries of Christ,
Teacher in the way of hidden service, *pray for us*

St David Lewis, Faithful father of the poor and needy,
Teacher in the way of Christ-like tenderness, *pray for us*

Bl Edward Powell, Wise soul and defender of the innocent,
Teacher in the way of Truth, *pray for us*

Bl William Gunter, Victim of ungodly vengeance,
Teacher in the way of forgiveness, *pray for us*

Bl Richard Flower, Young apostle and servant of the
   Church,
Teacher in the way of zeal, *pray for us*

Bl Humphrey Pritchard, Humble guardian of the weak,
Teacher in way of generosity, *pray for us*

Bl Edward Jones, Eloquent preacher of the Word of God,
Teacher in the way of the Gospel, *pray for us*

Bl William Davies, Guide of those who seek Christ,
Teacher in the way of discernment, *pray for us*

Bl Philip Powel, Servant of the servants of Christ,
Teacher in the way of reverence, *pray for us*

Lamb of God, who takes away the sins of the world,
Spare us, O Lord.
Lamb of God, who takes away the sins of the world,
Graciously hear us, O Lord.

Lamb of God, who takes away the sins of the world,
Have mercy on us.

Pray for us, you holy martyrs of God,
That we may be made worthy of the promises of Christ.
Let us pray

Almighty Lord and Father you raise up your devoted sons, the Martyrs of Wales, for their constancy in faith, generosity in love and dedication to your Holy Church. Grant through their intercession that we your people may grow in holiness and joy, imitating their example and seeking the reconciliation of all your children. We ask this through Christ our Lord. Amen.

Novena of Humility
Through the intercession of Blessed Humphrey Pritchard

O Blessed Humphrey,
pray that I may rejoice in the truth
and recognise my miserable state
but also God's loving mercy
in which he seeks to raise me up
in true holiness.
Obtain for me the grace
to be humble in all things,
to serve in all ways,
to desire the lowest place,
to remain hidden with Christ in God.
Amen.

Prayer to Blessed Richard Flower
For the young

Blessed Richard,
fervent patron of the young,
take to your heart the young people of our time
and guide them on the path of the Gospel.
Help them in the challenges that they face
and intercede for their needs.
May they be filled with that zeal
which marked your life
and made you a devoted son of the Church.
Teach them virtue and patience,
understanding and faithfulness,
purity and forbearance,
gentleness and self-control.
Lead them on the path to holiness,
committed to the truth,
and heroic in the ways of the Lord.

Pray for them, Blessed Richard;
That they may be made worthy of the promises of Christ.

Let us pray

Almighty and eternal God, you called your blessed martyr, St Richard Flower, to lay down his life while yet in the springtime of his youth. Through his intercession grant every grace and blessing to our young people, draw them to yourself, that they may come to share in the joys you have laid up for your faithful people. We ask this through Christ our Lord. Amen.

A Year with the English Saints

Fr Nicholas Schofield, Fr Gerard Skinner and Fr Richard Whinder

This booklet offers brief biographies of the saints of the English calendar, as well as suggestions of places to visit in connection with each saint and quotations from the saint's own writings. It combines familiar saints such as Thomas Beckett and Edward the Confessor with less familiar ones from the nation's history – among them Wulstan, Alban, Etheldreda, Hilda. Also included are brief biographies of the saints of Wales. These holy men and women remind us both of our rich native Christian heritage, and of the Church in England's links with the wider Catholic Church.

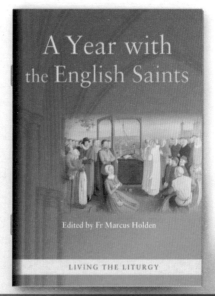

B756   ISBN 978 1 86082 886 7

A Handbook of Scriptural Novenas
For Various Needs & Intentions

These newly composed novena prayers present figures from Scripture from whom we learn lessons in faith and prayer. The situations and difficulties they faced frequently mirror our own worries and concerns. Thus Hannah prays for the gift of children, Job learns to be honest with God, Martha complains that she does all the work, Deborah and Barak learn what to do when overwhelmed, and Jonah too when God's plan doesn't seem to make sense. These and other figures open the Scriptures to us, and we learn more of the Novenas as a form of prayer.

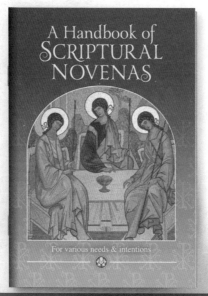

D798 ISBN: 978 1 78469 066 3

Has this book helped you?
Spread the word!

@CTSpublishers

/CTSpublishers

ctscatholiccompass.org

Let us know!
marketing@ctsbooks.org
+44 (0)207 640 0042

Learn, love, live your faith.
www.CTSbooks.org